October

Mary Ann,

Perhaps when you have a cup
of tea (or coffee) you'll think
of me and how very much I
value your friendship.

Happy 70th Birthday
and many more,
Sandi

THE Art of Tea and Friendship

Savoring the Fragrance of Time Together

PAINTINGS BY

Sandy Lynam Clough®

HARVEST HOUSE® PUBLISHERS

EUGENE, OREGON

The Art of Tea and Friendship

Copyright © 2003 by Sandy Lynam Clough
Published by Harvest House Publishers
Eugene, Oregon 97402
www.harvesthousepublishers.com

Library of Congress Cataloging-in-Publication Data

Clough, Sandy Lynam, 1948-
  The art of tea and friendship / artwork by Sandy Lynam Clough.
      p. cm.
   ISBN-13: 978-0-7369-1098-9
   ISBN-10: 0-7369-1098-0 (alk. paper)
 I. Afternoon teas. 2. Tea. 3. Entertaining. I. Title.
  TX736.C64 2003
  641.5'3—dc21

                         2003001827

Design and production by Garborg Design Works, Minneapolis, Minnesota

Harvest House Publishers has made every effort to trace the ownership of all poems and quotes. In the event of a question arising from the use of a poem or quote, we regret any error made and will be pleased to make the necessary correction in future editions of this book.

Printed in Hong Kong

08 09 10 / NG / 10 9 8

With great joy, I painted the tea and friendship found in this book just for you. How happily the time flew by as I created every thread of lace, sparkle of pretty china, and delicate rose petal. In these pages I not only included the beautiful "tea things" that express our femininity so well, but I also dipped the paintbrush of my heart into the glow of kindred hearts, into the light and fragrance of true friendship, to set the scene for you.

There is an art to sharing tea and friendship. Every woman, young or old, has this artistic gift. The warmth of caring and the joy in our hearts cause us to create friendships by giving of ourselves.

Tea makes a very good "paintbrush" for friendship. As you serve tea, "dip" it into the teatime "colors" of shared joy and genuine concern, and "mix in" loveliness of spirit. What a beautiful scene you are creating! Listening, laughter, tears, and loyalty are all part of a friendship "masterpiece."

If you enjoy tea and friendship, I invite you to join Sandy's Tea Society— a place where we encourage one another with a continuous supply of creative ideas. Members of Sandy's Tea Society have shared their teatime ideas as gifts of inspiration to you in this very book. We would welcome your company! Please visit us at www.sandysteasociety.com as we join kindred hearts with a cup of friendship.

Sandy Lynam Clough

I'm sending you love and tea,
To warm your winter's day.
Think of me as you pour your cup
And all the good things we would say.
If we could be together now
Instead of miles apart,
We'd sip our teas and memories,
The sweet warmth fills the heart.

SUSAN YOUNG

Somehow, taking tea together encourages an atmosphere of intimacy
when you slip off the timepiece in your mind and cast your fate to a
delight of tasty tea, tiny foods, and thoughtful conversation.

GAIL GRECO

There are few hours in life more
dedicated to the ceremony known

Teapot is on, the cups are waiting,

Favorite chairs anticipating,

No matter what I have to do,

My friend, there's always time for you.

AUTHOR UNKNOWN

agreeable than the hour

as afternoon tea.

HENRY JAMES

*E*very month my sister-in-law and I would take turns planning an afternoon out for tea at various tea shops in and around our city. We enjoyed many different tea experiences from the Victorian to the Japanese. Several years later, I had to move out-of-state but we still talk of our teatimes together. Now in my new city, I enjoy introducing my new friends to the tea experience that I so cherished and enjoyed with my sister-in-law.

PAULA PETRY
Albuquerque, NM

Sandy Lynam Clough

Afternoon Tea should be
provided, fresh supplies,
with thin bread-and-butter,
fancy pastries, cakes, etc.,
being brought in as other
guests arrive.

MRS. BEETON
The Book of Household Management

*When we honestly ask ourselves
which person in our lives means
the most to us, we often find that it
is those who, instead of giving
advice, solutions, or cures, have
chosen rather to share our pain and
touch our wounds with a warm and
tender hand. The friend who can be
silent with us in a moment of despair
or confusion, who can stay with us in
an hour of grief and bereavement,
who can tolerate not knowing, not
curing, not healing and face with
us the reality of our powerlessness,
that is a friend who cares.*

HENRI NOUWEN

Sandy Lynam Clough

Afternoon Tea

My copper kettle whistles merrily

and signals that it's time for tea.

The fine china cups are filled with the brew.

There's lemon and sugar and sweet cream, too.

But, best of all there's friendship, between you and me.

As we lovingly share our afternoon tea.

MARIANNA JO AROLIN

*I*n nothing more is the English genius for domesticity more notably declared than in the institution of this festival— almost one may call it—of afternoon tea...The mere chink of cups and saucers tunes the mind to happy repose.

GEORGE GISSING
The Private Papers of Henry Ryecroft

The tea party is a spa for the soul. You leave your

Busy people forget their business. Your stress melts

$\mathcal{M}$eanwhile, let us have a sip of tea. The afternoon glow is brightening the bamboos, the fountains are bubbling with delight, the soughing of the pines is heard in our kettle. Let us dream of evanescence, and linger in the beautiful foolishness of things.

OKAKURA KAKUZO

cares and work behind.

away, your senses awaken...

ALEXANDRA STODDARD

$\mathcal{F}$riendship $\mathcal{T}$opiary

Materials needed:
1 vintage teacup and saucer
1 small foam ball
1 medium foam ball
1 $\frac{1}{4}$-inch dowel about 6 inches long
$\frac{3}{4}$ cup scented loose leaf tea (such as jasmine or rose)
1 12-inch piece of sheer ribbon
Spanish moss
tacky glue
glue gun

Directions:
1. Cut small foam ball in half. Place one half cut-side down in teacup. Trim to fit. If loose, secure with dab of hot glue.
2. Pour loose leaf tea onto a paper plate. Brush tacky glue over medium foam ball. Roll in tea to cover completely. Set aside to dry.
3. Insert dowel into middle of teacup. Put a dab of hot glue on tip of the dowel. Place tea-covered ball securely on top of the dowel.
4. Tie ribbon into a soft bow. Secure to top of topiary with a dab of hot glue.
5. Brush small foam ball in teacup with tacky glue. Attach moss to cover. Set aside to dry.

There is always a great deal of poetry and fine sentiment in a chest of tea.

RALPH WALDO EMERSON

The year my daughter graduated from high school, I decided to have a graduation tea party for her and invited some special women who had been influential in her life. In the invitation, I asked everyone to bring a teacup and saucer that would represent them to give as a special gift for Haley. Each person took a turn telling why they brought their unique cup. The stories they shared about Haley were wonderful. There were lots of tears and lots of laughter. I bought handkerchiefs at a second-hand store for a small token of remembrance for each guest. I knew they would be needed. We have used those cups and saucers several times since then for other tea parties, and every time we reminisce about the party and each woman who made my daughter who she is today.

NANCY PROCTOR
Swisher, IA

Did You Know?

The term *orange-pekoe* (which is the most widely distributed type of tea) refers to the location of the tea leaves on the actual plant. It has nothing to do with the citrus fruit. Orange-pekoe leaves are the second branch of leaves from the top of the *Camellia sinensis* tea plant.

There is no trouble so great or grave that cannot be much diminished by a nice cup of tea.

BERNARD-PAUL HEROUX

Why, the club was just
the quietest place in the
world, a place where a
woman could run in to
brush her hair and wash
her hands, and change her
library book, and have a
cup of tea. A few of them
had formed it years ago,
just half a dozen of them,
at a luncheon; it was like
a little family circle, one
knew everybody there, and
one felt at home there.

KATHLEEN THOMPSON NORRIS
Saturday's Child

The most I can do for my friend

is simply be his friend.

HENRY DAVID THOREAU

Black Currant Iced Tea

6 black currant tea bags
2 cups boiling water
$1/4$ cup sugar
3 cups cold water
cranberry juice
ice

Pour boiling water over tea bags. Steep 90 seconds; then remove bags. Stir in sugar and cold water. Add splash of cranberry juice and ice. Enjoy with a friend on a hot summer's day.

$\mathcal{I}$ smile, of course,

And go on drinking tea,

Yet with these April sunsets, that somehow recall

My buried life, and Paris in the Spring,

I feel immeasurably at peace, and find the world

To be wonderful and youthful, after all.

T.S. ELIOT

There is one friend in the life of each of us, who seems not a separate person, however dear and beloved, but an expansion, an interpretation, of one's self, the very meaning of one's soul.

EDITH WHARTON

For the past 15 years, I have hosted a Christmas tea on the Monday before Christmas. I enclose a postcard in with our family Christmas card. It is always good to relax with a cup of tea during the busy holiday season. I serve tea and everyone brings something small to snack on. We have an under $5 gift, hopefully something handmade, and my husband helps pass them out. It is a fun girls' night out with time to catch up on the past year. Sometimes we cry, some years are harder than others, but mostly we laugh and enjoy each other's friendship.

TERI KONIECKI
Philadelphia, PA

The spirit of the tea beverage is one of peace, comfort, and refinement.

ARTHUR GRAY

Sandy Lynam Clough

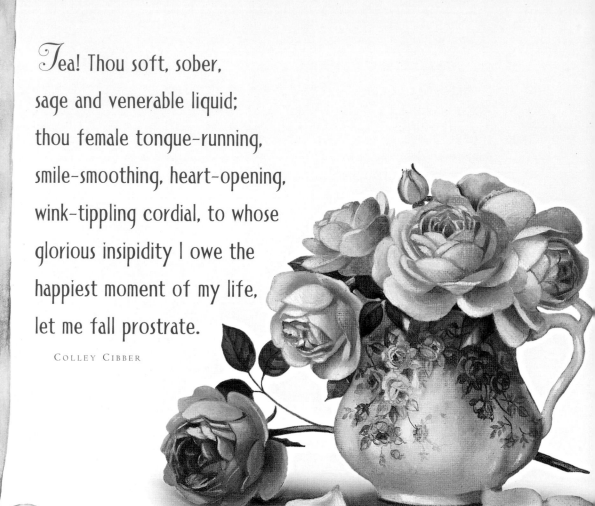

Tea! Thou soft, sober,
sage and venerable liquid;
thou female tongue-running,
smile-smoothing, heart-opening,
wink-tippling cordial, to whose
glorious insipidity I owe the
happiest moment of my life,
let me fall prostrate.

COLLEY CIBBER

"It's your birthday tea, Bert," said Mrs. Perks,
"and here's an ounce of your extry particular.
I got it o' Saturday along o' your happening to
remember it was your birthday to-day."

EDITH NESBIT
The Railway Children

Now stir the fire, and close the shutters fast,

Let fall the curtains, wheel the sofa round,

And, while the bubbling and loud hissing urn

Throws up a steamy column and the cups

That cheer but not inebriate, wait on each,

So let us welcome peaceful ev'ning in.

WILLIAM COWPER

Friends are kisses blown to us by angels.

AUTHOR UNKNOWN

A couple of years ago, two ladies who were homeschooling started getting together on Tuesdays at 2:00 for tea and to give their children a chance to visit with each other. After a long day of homeschooling, it's nice to take one afternoon a week for yourself, to relax and have an adult conversation!

They did this for about a year. It was such a special time for them, so they invited another homeschool mom to join them. She enjoyed it as well. Two months later, she invited me to join them. We take turns each week being the hostess. We always use our best dishes and linens. This always makes everyone feel special.

Our little girls are invited to join us as well. I feel it's so important to have them in this special atmosphere! One of my daughters likes to sit and sip with us the whole afternoon. My other daughter likes to sit and sip a while, then go play with the boys.

We only have one rule — no gossip! We are all very refreshed by the end of our teatime because our conversations are only positive. We each have a wonderful husband that sees how important this time is for us. We are better wives and mothers when we have this time to relax and do something special for ourselves. Tuesday has become the most favorite day of our week!

CHRISTIANE CARTER
Bennett, CO

Sandy Lynam Clough

The cozy fire is bright and gay,
The merry kettle boils away
And hums a cheerful song.
I sing the saucer and the cup;
Pray, Mary, fill the teapot up,
And do not make it strong.

BARRY PAIN

The naming of teas is a difficult matter,
It isn't just one of your everyday games—
Some might think you as mad as a hatter
Should you tell them each goes by several names.
For starters each tea in this world must belong
To the families Black or Green or Oolong;
Then look more closely at these family trees—
Some include Indians along with Chinese.

T.S. ELIOT

I keep a list of names of friends and women I don't get to see on a regular basis. I try to keep in touch with them by a cheerful phone call, a card, or an invitation to my home for tea. We are all so busy, but my list reminds me to reach out and encourage them regularly. It's wonderful to know someone is thinking of you!

LISA LEWIS
West Pittston, PA

27

There is magic in long-distance friendships.
They let you relate to other human beings
in a way that goes beyond being physically
together and is often more profound.

DIANA CORTES

A combination of fine tea, enchanting objects and soothing surroundings exerts a therapeutic effect by washing away the corrosive strains and stress of modern life...[it] induces a mood that is spiritually refreshing...[and produces] a genial state of mind.

JOHN BLOFELD

*I*t is amazing what a portable tea for one can do to lift someone's spirit. I take a basket or gift bag with a mug filled with a variety of tea bags, scones or mini muffins from the bakery, a tiny jar of jelly, and a few sugar cubes wrapped up in a handkerchief to a sick friend, an elderly house-bound neighbor, or a new mother. I tell them to sit and enjoy it when they feel the need for a hug or to relax. It never fails to bring a smile.

SHERRIE STYLES
Titusville, FL

*A true friend reaches
for your hand and
touches your heart.*

AUTHOR UNKNOWN

When the girl returned, some hours later, she carried a tray, with a cup of fragrant tea steaming on it; and a plate piled up with very hot buttered toast, cut thick, very brown on both sides, with the butter running through the holes in it in great golden drops, like honey from the honeycomb. The smell of that buttered toast simply talked to Toad, and with no uncertain voice; talked of warm kitchens, of breakfasts on bright frosty mornings, of cosy parlour firesides on winter evenings, when one's ramble was over and slippered feet were propped on the fender; of the purring of contented cats, and the twitter of sleepy canaries. Toad sat up on end once more, dried his eyes, sipped his tea and munched his toast, and soon began talking freely about himself, and the house he lived in, and his doings there, and how important he was, and what a lot his friends thought of him.

KENNETH GRAHAME
Wind in the Willows

If you are cold, tea will warm you;
If you are too heated, it will cool you;
If you are depressed, it will cheer you;
If you are excited, it will calm you.

WILLIAM GLADSTONE

My dear, if you could give me a cup
of tea to clear my muddle of a head
I should better understand your affairs.

CHARLES DICKENS

The cup of tea on arrival at a country house is a thing which, as a rule, I particularly enjoy. I like the crackling logs, the shaded lights, the scent of buttered toast, the general atmosphere of leisured coziness.

P.G. WODEHOUSE
The Code of the Woosters

This is a special tea for children. It is a way to introduce a charitable act, encourage a new friendship, and be selfless.

At this tea party, we bake gingerbread cookies and treats, make Christmas-related crafts and small gifts, and then donate them to either a nursing home or to the children's ward at the hospital. It is truly a delight to see the smiles that this tea brings for all involved.

DEBRA GALLEGOS
Baton Rouge, LA

I recently had a special tea for a woman on another farm, some miles away from me. She is a single mom with three children, one a newborn. She was feeling very lonely and discouraged. Over the phone, my mind began ticking about what I could do on the spur of the moment, so I said, "Come on over." I did not even promise a tea, but by the time she arrived, I had set the table and loaded the three-tiered serving dishes with sliced fruits and vegetables, sliced meats, cheese, and a quick batch of scones with whipping cream and jam. I included an empty jar filled with sage, roses, and forget-me-nots freshly cut from my flowerbed.

While she sat in what I call my "Peacock Chair," a large wicker piece with a high back, I went to fetch my sparkly tiara, which I keep stored in a hat box among gloves and corsages. I brought out the tiara, placed it on her head, and she wore it the entire party. I snapped several pictures of her with it. I noticed her countenance lifted quite soon after she wore the tiara. I thought that headpiece was rather useless sitting in a box, and it gave her such a thrill to wear it and to be "Princess for a Day" that I have decided to make this a regular ceremony in my life with any woman who needs a bit of kindness. I learned quickly that one needs to have tea things always in stock so she can "throw together" a sudden tea party.

LYDIA SHERMAN
Junction City, OR

She poured out Swann's tea, inquired "Lemon or cream?" and, on his answering "Cream, please," said to him with a laugh: "A cloud!" And as he pronounced it excellent, "You see, I know just how you like it." This tea had indeed seemed to Swann, just as it seemed to her, something precious, and love has such a need to find some justification for itself, some guarantee of duration, in pleasures which without it would have no existence and must cease with its passing...

MARCEL PROUST
Swann's Way

And so it continued all day, wynde after wynde, from a room beyond came the whistle of a teakettle. "Now, you really must join me. I've some marvelous Darjeeling, and some delicious petit fours a friend of mine gave me for Christmas."

MARTHA GRIMES
The Man with a Load of Mischief

My sister-in-law mailed my daughter and I our own tea-party invitation. It instructed us to set up a tea party on our end, as simple or elaborate as we chose. She would then set up a tea party on her end. At a specific date and time, she would call us and we would talk on the telephone and have our tea party—long distance! (She lives in Idaho, and we live in Missouri.) My daughter and I each brought a special guest (a doll), and Elaine had a special doll as a guest at her tea party as well. We took pictures throughout our tea party to exchange with each other.

Now we know of a great way to stay close and catch up on each other's lives via long distance tea parties. We are planning to have another around Christmas because we are unable to spend the holidays together.

GINGER ENGLISH
St. Charles, MO

If instead of a gem, or even a flower, we should cast the gift of a loving thought into the heart of a friend, that would be giving as the angels give.

GEORGE MACDONALD

Each cup of tea represents an imaginary voyage.

CATHERINE DOUZEL

I invited eight special friends and their daughters over for a Valentine's Tea. At this tea, I asked each to invite three new friends who we did not know to complete their table at the upcoming May tea. It was to be called the May Mystery Tea with the theme "The Language of Flowers." Each friend was asked to choose a favorite flower to be featured on their table. The tables featured violets, lilies, wildflowers, hydrangeas, and roses. (My friend used the yellow rose tea set that her mother gave her right before she passed away. The tea set had not been taken out of the box until that tea. Now the tea set has been passed to the teenage daughter to set her first tea table.) The tables on the lush lawn were beautifully adorned with the assorted chosen flowers. The backs of chairs donned the featured flower wrapped in toile of spring colors. The cake featured violets with the inscription, "Violets for Faithfulness." Many new friends were made that warm spring day, and we all look forward to the annual May tea.

SANDY MCGUIRE
Lilburn, GA

Sandy Lynam Clough

"*I can just imagine myself
sitting down at the head of the
table and pouring out the tea,*"
*said Anne, shutting her eyes
ecstatically, "and asking
Diana if she takes sugar!
I know she doesn't but
of course I'll ask her
just as if I didn't know.*"

L.M. MONTGOMERY
Anne of Green Gables

Sandy Lynam Clough

To remind my friends how special they are to me, I gave each woman at the tea party a small keepsake. There was a wooden teapot placed at the left-hand corner of each place-mat. I painted and personalized each one and filled them with little scrolls that had inspirational blessings inside. The guests were encouraged to pour themselves a cup of blessings whenever things get a little tough and they need to know that they are not alone.

CHRISTY KILGORE
Duluth, MN

Christopher Robin was home by this time, because it was the afternoon, and he was so glad to see them that they stayed there until very nearly tea-time, and then they had a *Very Nearly* tea, which is one you forget about afterwards, and hurried on to Pooh Corner, so as to see Eeyore before it was too late to have a *Proper Tea* with Owl.

A.A. MILNE
The House at Pooh Corner

I wish we could sit down together,

And have a cup of tea,

But since we can't

When you have this one,

I hope you'll think of me.

AUTHOR UNKNOWN

Through my book club, I met two young ladies who are being homeschooled. They had expressed an interest in learning more about tea. I told them I would be delighted to have a "home economics" lesson and invited them, along with a few other book club ladies, to my home for a tea. Because the tea was being held on a school day (and I am a former teacher) I wrote a lesson plan, "Giving Your First Tea," and included all the important elements of planning and hosting a tea. We decided the most important thing about giving a tea is to make sure your guests are having a good time and not to worry too much about doing everything exactly right. Also, keep your menu simple so that you are not too exhausted to enjoy the tea yourself. One of my guests surprised the girls by giving them floral teacups to take home and start their own collections of tea "necessities." Within two days, I received charming, handmade thank-you notes from the girls thanking all of us for the home economics lesson on "Giving Your First Tea."

PAT BORYSIEWICZ
Ocoee, FL

I invited seven friends to an informal garden tea party. I asked them to wear a straw hat and their garden clothes and to bring a rooted cutting or seeds from their garden for the friendship garden I've started. I painted a 6-inch flowerpot and filled it with flowers for each of them to take home.

SHEILA SCHOLOTTERBECK
Chanute, KS

*C*ynthia came in quietly and set a cup of tea before him. He kissed her hand, inexpressibly grateful, and she went back into the kitchen. When we view the little things with thanksgiving, even they become big things.

JAN KARON
These High, Green Hills

You can never get a cup of tea large enough or a book long enough to suit me.

C.S. LEWIS

There is no trouble so great or grave that cannot be much diminished by a nice cup of tea.

BERNARD-PAUL HEROUX

*M*ay your home always be too small for all your friends," reads a plaque in my friend's house. I once lived in a home that was so small that a guest remarked, "I can't believe real people live here!"

Even if your home is too small to host all of your friends at one time, you can throw open the doors and welcome them all with a "Come and Go" Tea Party, an idea I learned from my mother.

By staggering the times on your invitations, you can enjoy all your friends at one special party. Invite one-third of your guests to tea from 1-3 P.M., one-third from 2-4 P.M., and one-third from 3-5 P.M.

Enlist the help of two or three friends to serve the food and tea and clear the tables so you can be sure to be available at the door for every "Hello" and "Goodbye." Be sure to be cautious about food safety and replace all the food every two hours. An electric coffee urn with fresh hot water will help keep the teapots filled.

Not only will you enjoy seeing so many friends together, each of them is sure to find some new friends at your house!

SANDY LYNAM CLOUGH
Marietta, GA

May this tea be steeped with love

For friendships sent down from above.

SANDY LYNAM CLOUGH